Floral Cross-Stitch

Eleanore Gross-Ekowski

Sterling Publishing Co., Inc.   New York

Translated by Elisabeth E. Reinersmann
Drawings by Ekkehard Dreschel
Photographs by Thomas A. Weiss
Edited by Claire Wilson

Library of Congress Cataloging-in-Publication Data

Gross-Ekowski, Eleanore.
    Floral cross-stitch / by Eleanore Gross-Ekowski ; [translated by
Elisabeth E. Reinersmann ; drawings by Ekkehard Dreschel ;
photographs by Thomas A. Weiss].
            p.   cm.
    A compilation of two titles originally published in German as:
Frühlingsblumen and Blütenträume in Kreuztich.
    Includes index.
    ISBN 0-8069-8312-4
    1. Cross-stitch—Patterns.   2. Decoration and ornament—Plant
forms.   I. Title.
TT778.C76G77   1991
746.44'3041—dc20   90-28448
                                                         CIP

10 9 8 7 6 5 4 3 2 1

English translation and editorial compilation © 1991
by Sterling Publishing Company, Inc.
387 Park Avenue South, New York, N.Y. 10016
This is a compilation of two titles originally published
as *Frühlingsblumen* © 1988 and *Blütenträume* © 1991
by Ravensburger Buchverlag Otto Maier GmbH
Distributed in Canada by Sterling Publishing
% Canadian Manda Group, P.O. Box 920, Station U
Toronto, Ontario, Canada M8Z 5P9
Distributed in Great Britain and Europe by Cassell PLC
Villiers House, 41/47 Strand, London WC2N 5JE
Distributed in Australia by Capricorn Ltd.
P.O. Box 665, Lane Cove, NSW 2066
Printed in Hong Kong,
Produced by Mandarin Offset.
6th Floor, 22A Westlands Road,
Quarry Bay, Hong Kong.
All rights reserved.

Sterling ISBN 0-8069-8312-4

INTRODUCTION

Cross-stitch has been a popular method of decorating fabric for generations. The reasons for this are simple—cross-stitch is easy to master, it requires very little investment, and many designs can be finished relatively quickly. All that you really need to start out are a simple pattern, some embroidery floss, a piece of linen, and a proper needle. If you like, you can also purchase a pair of scissors and an embroidery frame to make things a little easier.

MATERIALS

All of the samplers in this book are stitched on either #10.5 or #12 linen, which means that the fabric contains either 10.5 or 12 threads per square centimeter. Simply look at the instruction section of each project to determine the appropriate size.

You may also choose to make your cross-stitch designs on *aida cloth*, which is specially made for this craft. Aida cloth consists of groups of threads that are woven into equal-sized squares. As a result, it is much easier to count your pattern out onto the material.

The projects in this book are shown in their finished form on each right-hand page in the pattern section. On each left-hand page, there is a corresponding graph with symbols that indicate the colors used in the project. Below each graph, a key tells you the color number to which each symbol refers. When you have determined the color numbers for your project, just look up the numbers in the color chart on pages 6 and 7 to see what the colors look like. (All of the color numbers in this book refer to MEZ embroidery floss. If you want to use either DMC or J. & P. Coates, just find a comparable number in the table on page 5.) When you have become familiar with cross-stitching, you can change colors to suit your individual taste.

Each square on the graph is equal to two threads on the linen, both horizontally and vertically. Keep in mind that the fewer threads per centimeter on the fabric, the larger the finished design will be. The opposite is true of fabric with more threads per inch.

EMBROIDERY FRAME

Frames come in several different sizes. Choose the one that feels most comfortable in your hand and that will best accommodate the size of your project. When mounting the linen in the frame, make sure that the threads run in a true vertical/horizontal direction to avoid distorting the material. You should leave the material in the frame only when you are actually working on your project. If you leave your work in the frame for any length of time, it will create a great deal of stress on the fabric.

NEEDLES AND EMBROIDERY FLOSS

The size of the needle that you use depends on your choice of material. The projects in this book were completed with a size 24 embroidery needle.

The MEZ floss used here is made of cotton and consists of six strands that are easily separated. Unless otherwise stated, use only two strands of floss at a time.

Note: It's a good idea to keep on hand a small pair of scissors to cut off ends of theads or to cut incorrect stitches.

Cross-stitching can be done either from left to right or up and down. In the left-to-right method, shown in diagram 1, the understitches are completed first. Each row of understitches runs diagonally across the fabric. The stitches start at the lower left corner of each box on the grid, pass over two threads, and end in the upper right corner of the box. The topstitches are made in the opposite direction, moving from the lower right corner to the upper left corner.

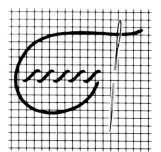 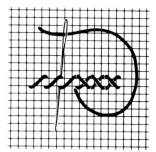

Diagram 2 illustrates the up-and-down method. Here, you create a vertical row of understitches, each of which runs from the lower left to the upper right of the box. Make the topstitches down the length of the row, stitching each from the upper right to the lower left.

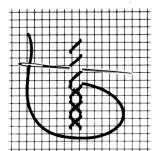 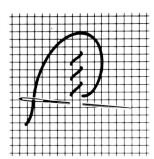

Note: Choose one method and stick with it. You should not switch methods in the middle of your work.

To begin stitching, determine the central point of both your pattern and area of the linen that you want to embroider. Mark this spot with a row of small basting stitches or with a dressmaker's marking pencil. Begin your stitching at this central point and work from left to right. Never start your design at the border because the chance of miscounting is too great.

TIPS

Here are a few tips to make your cross-stitching project easier:

To prevent the linen from unravelling as you work, make a ½-inch hem around the edges of the fabric.

When stitching leaves and blossoms, finish the veins first and then fill in the rest.

Secure the loose ends of the thread at the back of your work to keep the floss from tangling as you stitch. Do this by pulling the end underneath the back of the first 3 or 4 stitches.

FINISHING

A just-finished cross-stitch project usually does not look very good. If you did your stitching without a frame, the material will be creased and somewhat soiled. If you used a frame, there will be indentations and creases in the fabric.

In either case, it will be necessary to wash your embroidery. You should do this by hand and with only a minimum of detergent. You can then finish the piece in one of two ways—either stretch the wet material into shape and air-dry it on a flat surface or allow the material to dry as is and iron it into shape. However, if you use the second method, make sure you first place a damp towel on top of your work.

FRAMING

If you plan to frame your finished work, first cut a piece of cardboard one inch smaller around than the material. Then fold the excess material over the edges of the cardboard and secure it to the back with glue.

Cross-stitch samplers look best if they are set inside a photo mount and then framed. You may, of course, simply mount the piece behind glass in a standard frame.

If framing seems too difficult a task for you, then take your work to a frame shop and have the job professionally done.

The samplers in this book were all made with MEZ embroidery floss; the charts show the MEZ numbers. For those who prefer DMC or J. & P. Coats embroidery floss, the following numbers are suggested as possible alternatives.

MEZ	DMC	J. & P. COATS	MEZ	DMC	J. & P. COATS
1	Snow-white	1001	359	300	5349
2	ecru	1002	360	433	5471
6	948	2331	363	436	5943
8	754	2331	367	945	3335
9	819	3280	369	919	2326
10	3326	3126	370	434	5000
11	892	3152	371	433	5471
19	817	2335	373	435	5371
22	304	3401	374	434	5000
26	603	3001	375	436	5943
29	600	3056	378	435	5371
41	892	3152	381	938	5477
42	498	3410	382	898	5476
48	3689	3086	387	712	5387
49	776	3086	390	739	5369
50	963	3281	397	762	8510
59	815	3000	398	415	8510
68	326	3401	399	415	8510
75	3354	3003	400	414	8513
76	603	3001	401	413	8514
77	309	3284	403	310	8403
78	3350	3004	778	963	3280
95	211	4303	832	433	5471
98	550	4107	843	3012	6316
100	553	4097	844	471	6010
107	550	4107	846	938	5477
108	554	4104	847	762	8510
109	553	4097	848	415	8510
110	550	4107	850	932	7050
112	208	4301	851	823	7982
117	800	7021	853	840	5379
120	828	7053	854	640	5393
128	828	7053	856	434	5000
129	800	7021	860	3346	6258
130	809	7021	862	367	6018
131	799	7030	868	554	4104
132	796	7100	869	211	4303
133	824	7182	870	554	4104
146	825	7181	871	3687	3088
158	828	7053	872	902	3083
160	800	7021	876	320	6017
161	793	7977	878	701	6226
164	824	7182	880	745	2296
167	3325	7972	884	920	3337
185	747	7053	892	353	3006
188	993	6185	893	776	3281
300	744	2293	896	918	3340
302	725	2298	897	3685	3089
303	972	2307	901	783	2307
304	741	2314	903	780	2298
305	783	2307	905	838	5381
306	783	2307	920	809	7021
308	921	3336	921	809	7021
309	436	5943	922	311	3336
316	920	3337	926	739	5369
333	606	2334	928	828	7053
335	891	3254	939	809	7021
338	970	2327	941	825	7181
341	918	3340	943	782	2412
347	758	2337	972	815	3000
351	355	2339	975	747	7053
358	801	5475			

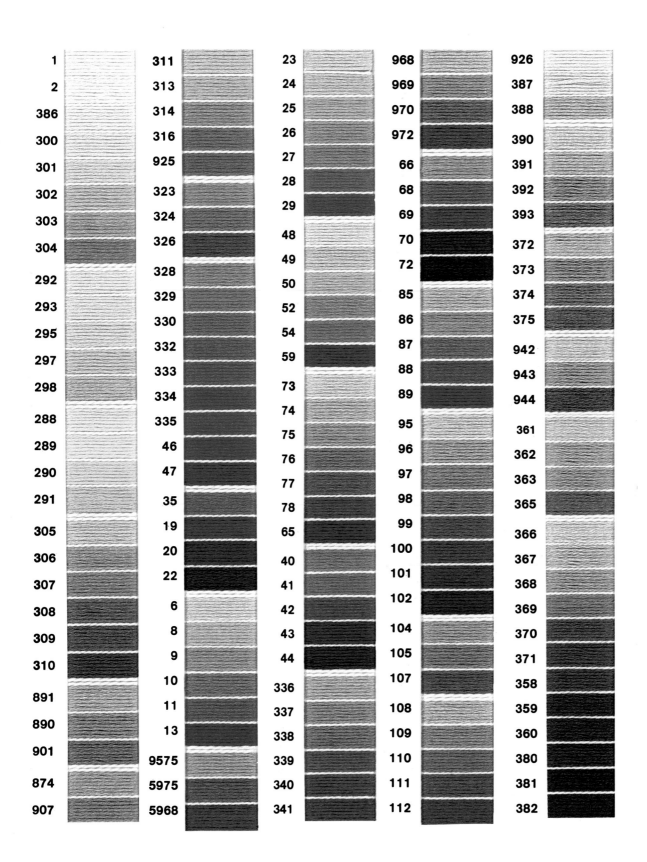

Color chart for MEZ embroidery floss

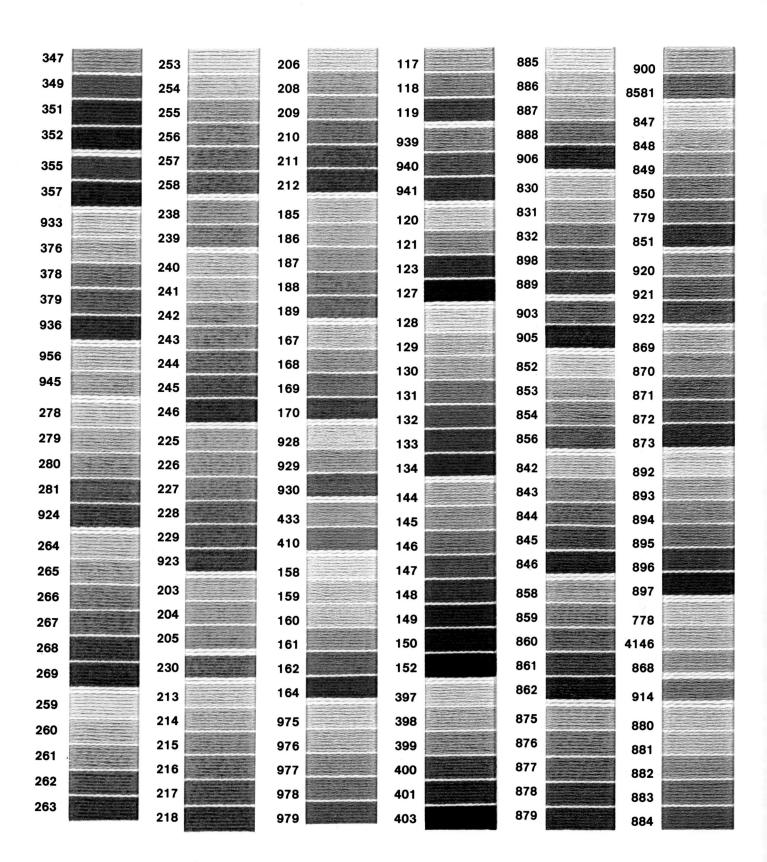

347
349
351
352
355
357
933
376
378
379
936
956
945
278
279
280
281
924
264
265
266
267
268
269
259
260
261
262
263

253
254
255
256
257
258
238
239
240
241
242
243
244
245
246
225
226
227
228
229
923
203
204
205
230
213
214
215
216
217
218

206
208
209
210
211
212
185
186
187
188
189
167
168
169
170
928
929
930
433
410
158
159
160
161
162
164
975
976
977
978
979

117
118
119
939
940
941
120
121
123
127
128
129
130
131
132
133
134
144
145
146
147
148
149
150
152
397
398
399
400
401
403

885
886
887
888
906
830
831
832
898
889
903
905
852
853
854
856
842
843
844
845
846
858
859
860
861
862
875
876
877
878
879

900
8581
847
848
849
850
779
851
920
921
922
869
870
871
872
873
892
893
894
895
896
897
778
4146
868
914
880
881
882
883
884

7

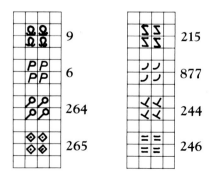

9		215
6		877
264		244
265		246

This small, delicate flower is one of the first to appear each year. It blooms as early as January in some regions and is characterized by narrow leaves and bell-shaped flowers.

SNOWDROP (*Galanthus nivalis*)

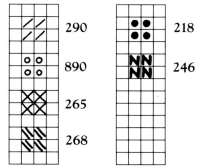

290	218	
890	246	
265		
268		

BACHELOR'S BUTTON
(Ranunculus acris)

*This flower is found almost every-
where, but most species are considered
weeds. Bachelor's button flowers in
early summer.*

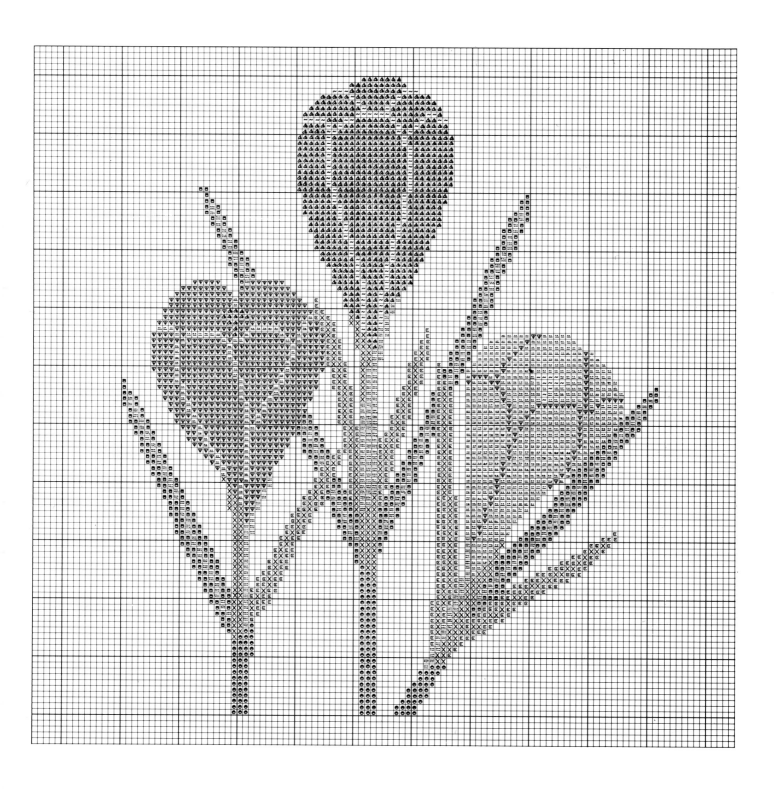

~ ~ / ~ ~ 297	◼ ◼ / ◼ ◼ 228	◉ ◉ / ◉ ◉ 859
▲ ▲ / ▲ ▲ 314	ⴲ ⴲ / ⴲ ⴲ 923	
▼ ▼ / ▼ ▼ 133	⠢ ⠢ / ⠢ ⠢ 842	
⠶ ⠶ / ⠶ ⠶ 102	X X / X X 858	

The crocus is the most common symbol of spring's approach. It comes in many colors, but the most popular varieties are purple and yellow.

CROCUS *(Crocus)*

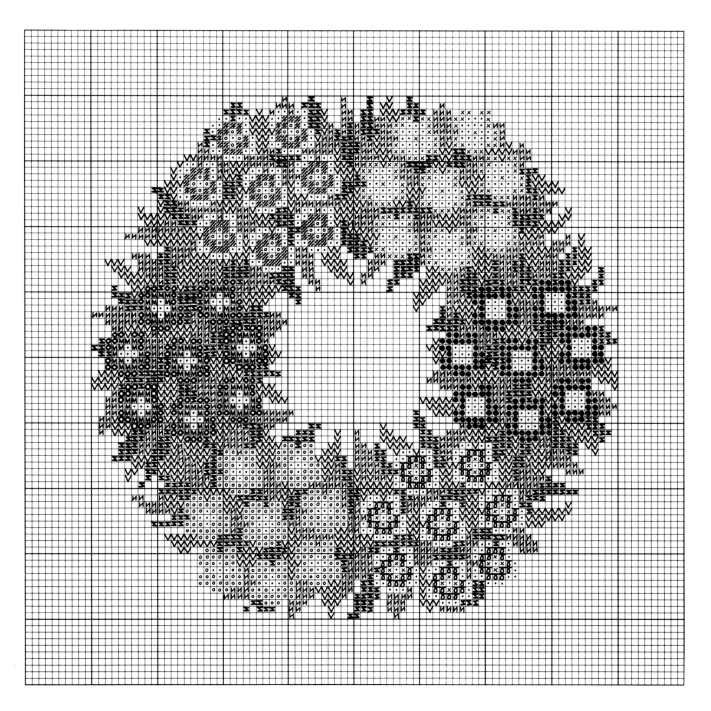

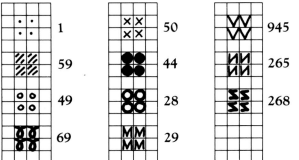

SWEET WILLIAM
(Dianthus barbatus)

This plant flowers between June and July and is closely related to the carnation and the pink.

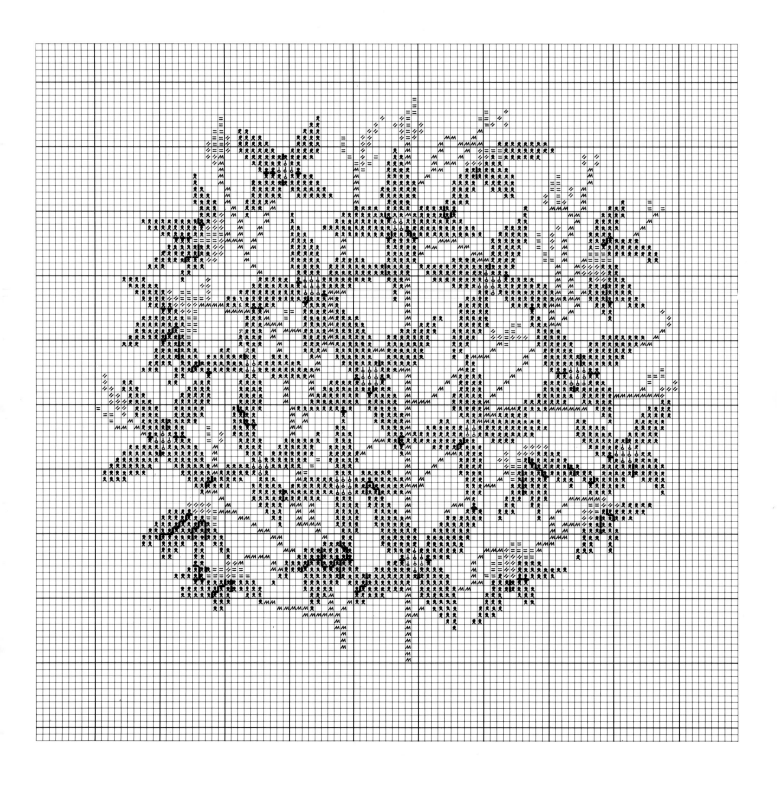

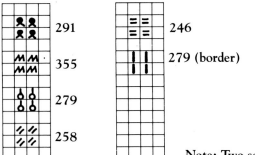

	291
	355
	279
	258

	246
	279 (border)

The forsythia is by far the best-known shrub and can be found in almost every yard. Its bell-shaped blossoms appear on bare branches in March or April.

Note: Two sets of #291 floss are needed for this project.

16

FORSYTHIA *(Forsythia)*

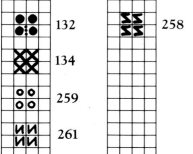

132	
134	
259	
261	
258	

LARKSPUR
(Delphinium consolida)
This tall plant produces giant spikes of
flowers between June and August.

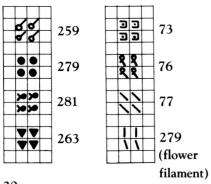

	259
	279
	281
	263

	73
	76
	77
	279 (flower filament)

	263 (endpoint of filament)

This flower received its name because of its bulb, which looks much like the tooth of a dog. It comes in many colors and blooms in March and April.

Note: Watch the direction of the filaments closely. In some cases, only one thread separates one from the other.

DOG'S-TOOTH VIOLET
(Erythronium dens-canis)

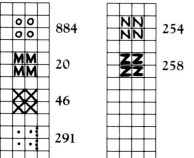

o o / o o	884
MM / MM	20
✕	46
• • / • •	291

NN / N	254
ZZ / ZZ	258

GAILLARDIA
(Gaillardia aristata)
The large blooms of this wildflower can sometimes reach 4 inches in diameter. Under the right conditions, it will flower from June to September.

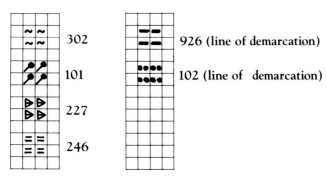

	302
	101
	227
	246

	926 (line of demarcation)
	102 (line of demarcation)

This plant is characterized by its heart-shaped leaves and rosette structure. It begins flowering in February and often continues into autumn.

VIOLET *(Viola odorata)*

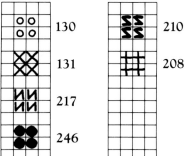

⊙⊙ ⊙⊙	130
⊠⊠ ⊠⊠	131
ИИ ИИ	217
●● ●●	246

⧉⧉ ⧉⧉	210
⊞ ⊞	208

CHICORY (*Cichoreum intybus*)

This plant is most commonly grown for its leaves, which are used in salads, and its roots, which are dried, ground, and added to coffee. However, chicory also produces lovely blue flowers during spring and can be grown as an ornamental garden plant.

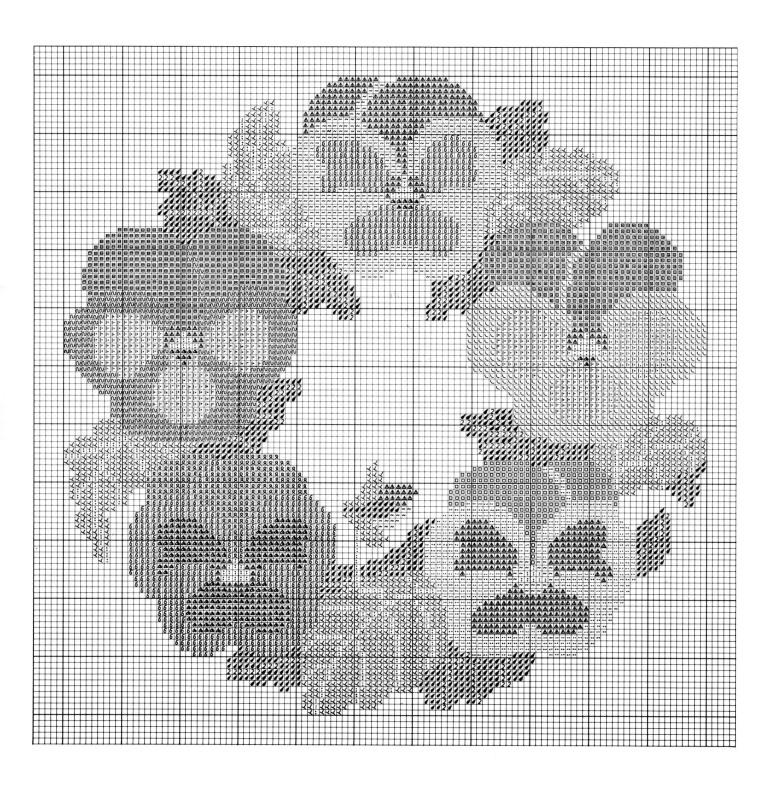

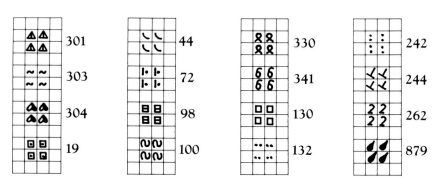

	301		44		330		242
	303		72		341		244
	304		98		130		262
	19		100		132		879

This is one of the most popular annual flowers and is found in almost every garden. If it is properly cared for, the pansy will bloom throughout much of the year.

PANSY *(Viola tricolor)*

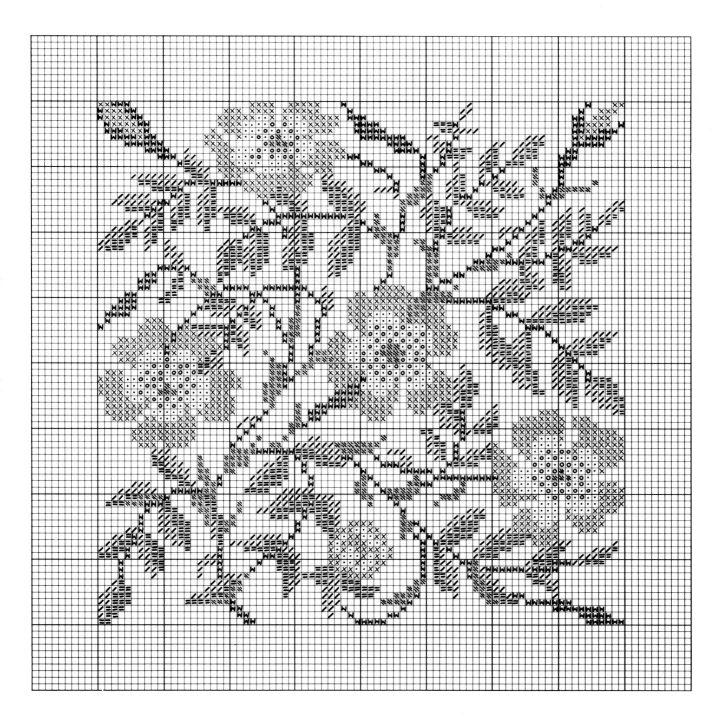

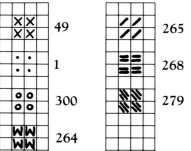

X X / X X	49	
• • / • •	1	
o o / o o	300	
W W / W W	264	

265	
268	
279	

DOG ROSE (*Rosa canina*)

The dog rose, a wild species, came by its strange name because the ancient Romans believed that it was a cure for rabies. It blooms for only a few weeks during May and June.

This modest but much admired plant is in bloom from March until June.

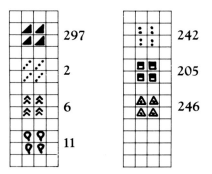

297	242
2	205
6	246
11	

DAISY *(Bellis perennis)*

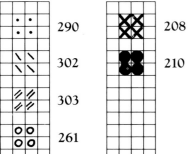

⠖	290
╲╲	302
╱╱	303
○○	261

⊗	208
⬤	210

DANDELION
(Taraxacum officinale)
This plant is usually thought of as a troublesome weed, but it is actually quite useful. Its leaves can be used in salads and in winemaking and its vivid yellow blossoms provide color during spring and summer.

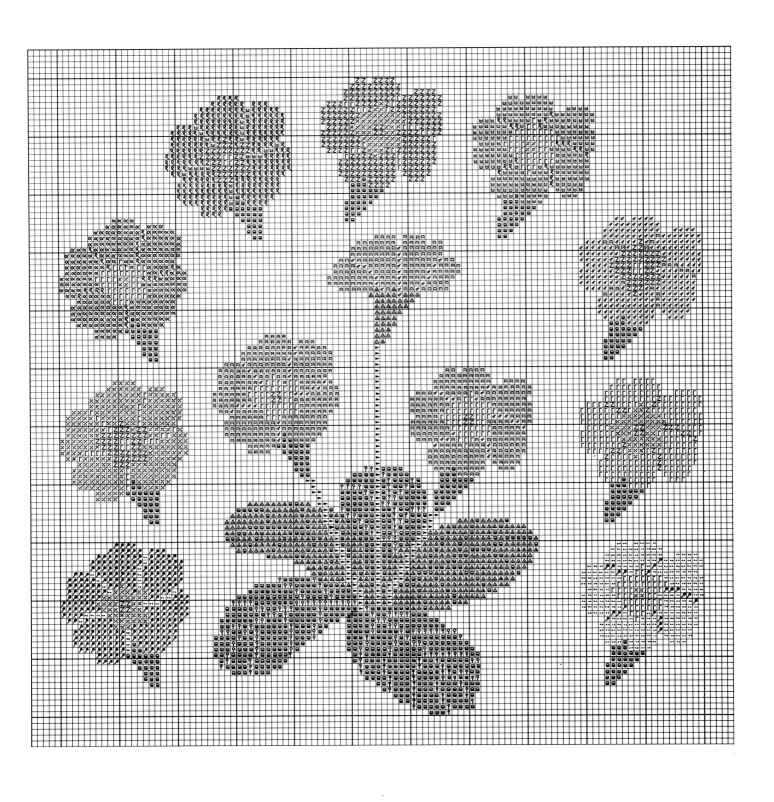

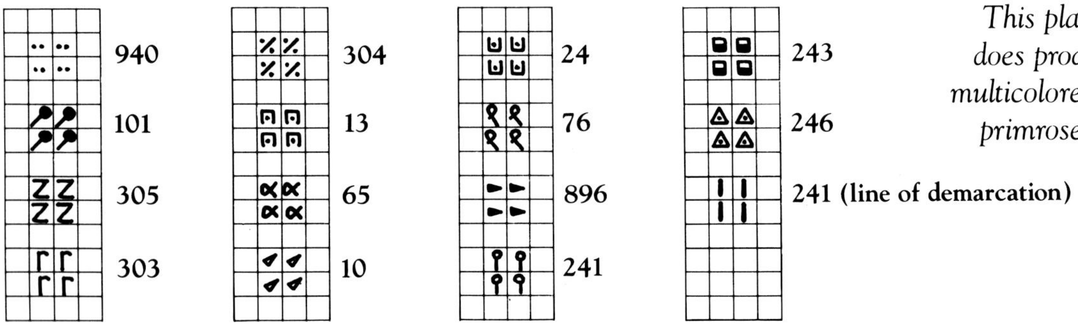

·· ·· ·· ··	940	
♪ ♪ ♪ ♪	101	
Z Z Z Z	305	
Γ Γ Γ Γ	303	

⁒ ⁒ ⁒ ⁒	304	
⋒ ⋒ ⋒ ⋒	13	
∝ ∝ ∝ ∝	65	
◢ ◢ ◢ ◢	10	

ப ப ப ப	24	
Ꝗ Ꝗ Ꝗ Ꝗ	76	
▶ ▶ ▶ ▶	896	
�የ �የ �የ �የ	241	

◘ ◘ ◘ ◘	243	
△ △ △ △	246	
‖ ‖ ‖ ‖	241 (line of demarcation)	

This plant is not a rose at all, but it does produce many different types of multicolored blossom. There are many primrose species, all of which bloom from March to July.

PRIMROSE *(Primula)*

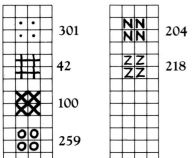

⊡ 301	⊞ 204
⊞ 42	⊞ 218
⊠ 100	
⊡ 259	

SPIDERWORT
(*Tradescantia virginiana*)
The vivid purple flowers of the spider-wort make it a popular garden plant. The blossoms appear in May or June and continue throughout the summer.

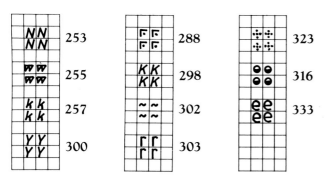

N N / N N	253	
ⱳ ⱳ / ⱳ ⱳ	255	
k k / k k	257	
Y Y / Y Y	300	

Γ Γ / Γ Γ	288	
K K / K K	298	
~ ~ / ~ ~	302	
Γ Γ / Γ Γ	303	

⁛ ⁛ / ⁛ ⁛	323	
◍ ◍ / ◍ ◍	316	
e e / e e	333	

After tulips, daffodils are among the most popular bulb plants. The bright golden blooms appear in March and last until the end of April.

DAFFODIL *(Narcissus)*

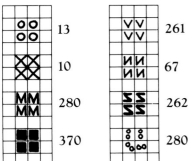

o o / o o	13	V V / V V	261
XX / XX	10	ИИ / ИИ	67
MM / MM	280	SS / SS	262
■■ / ■■	370	o o / o o	280

TURK'S-CAP LILY
(Lilium martagon)
Lilies are among the world's best-loved flowers. The Turk's-cap, with its strikingly dark flowers, blooms during June and July.

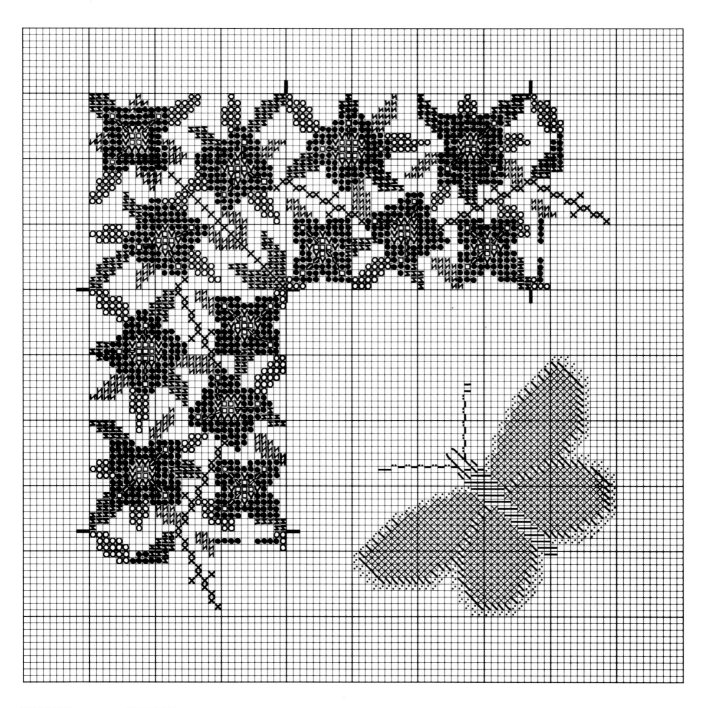

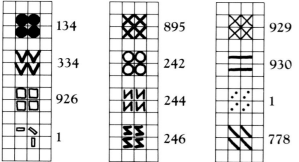

134	895	929	
334	242	930	
926	244	1	
1	246	778	

SPEEDWELL
(Veronica fruticans)

This plant's bright blue flowers, which sprout from large spikes, are a lovely sight. They appear in May and June and are very attractive to butterflies.

◇◇ ◇◇	265	🄰🄰 🄰🄰	13	ℤℤ ℤℤ	305
𝒽𝒽 𝒽𝒽	877	◊◊ ◊◊	208	𝖢𝖢 𝖢𝖢	306
○○ ○○	268	ℛℛ ℛℛ	324		
✿✿ ✿✿	441	ⅆⅆ ⅆⅆ	311†		

Tulips come in a dazzling number of varieties and colors. They all bloom during March and April.

TULIP *(Tulipa)*

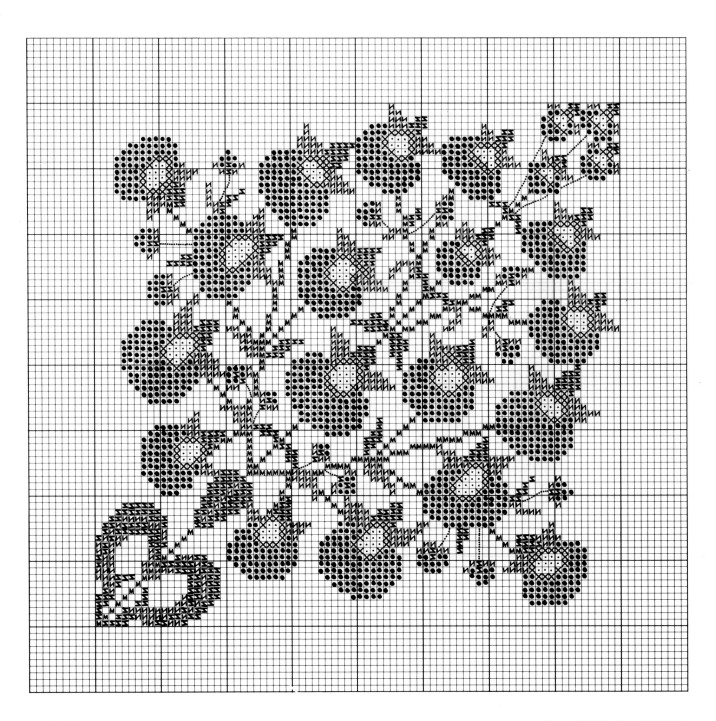

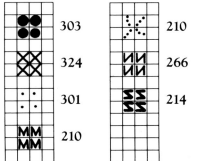

●● / ●●	303	
✖	324	
∴ / ∴	301	
MM / MM	210	

⠿	210	
ИИ / ИИ	266	
⧈⧈	214	

LADY'S SLIPPER
(Calceolaria integrifolia)
The strange, sacklike flowers of this plant come in either yellow or mottled and appear between June and October.

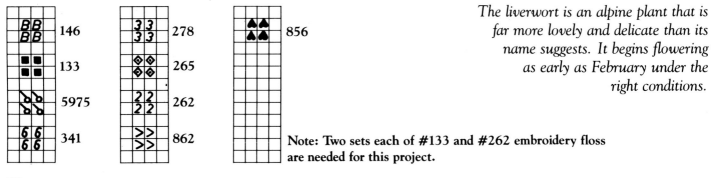

BB / BB	146	33 / 33	278	▲▲ / ▲▲ 856
■■ / ■■	133	◇◇ / ◇◇	265	
⬠⬠	5975	22 / 22	262	
66 / 66	341	>> / >>	862	

The liverwort is an alpine plant that is far more lovely and delicate than its name suggests. It begins flowering as early as February under the right conditions.

Note: Two sets each of #133 and #262 embroidery floss are needed for this project.

LIVERWORT (*Hepatica nobilis*)

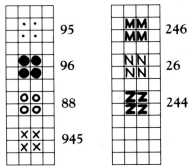

`··` `··`	95
`●●` `●●`	96
`oo` `oo`	88
`××` `××`	945

`MM` `MM`	246
`NN` `NN`	26
`ZZ` `ZZ`	244

GERMAN IRIS (*Iris germanica*)
The German or bearded iris is only one of the many types of plant in the iris family. It blooms in April, but other types of iris can bloom as early as February.

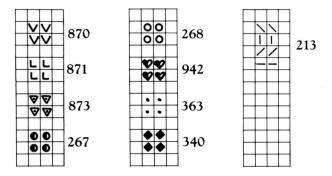

V V / V V	870
L L / L L	871
▽ ▽ / ▽ ▽	873
◐ ◐ / ◐ ◐	267

O O / O O	268
♥ ♥ / ♥ ♥	942
• • / • •	363
◆ ◆ / ◆ ◆	340

\ \ / | | / ╱ ╱ / ─ ─	213

This close relative of the Anemones is characterized by its blue flower, cup-shaped calyxes, and needlelike leaves.

PASQUEFLOWER *(Pulsatilla)*

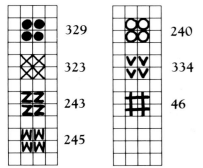

329	240
323	334
243	46
245	

ROSE (Rosa)

This is probably the most popular flower of all time. It comes in dozens of varieties and colors, some of which bloom only in spring and others that bloom throughout the summer.

This plant received its name because
its leaves bear a slight resemblance to
lung tissue. It blooms from March
until May.

♡ ♡	338	
♡ ♡		

Λ Λ	941	
Λ Λ		

⁞ ⁞	99	
⁞ ⁞		

◣ ◣	213	
◣ ◣		

A A	843	
A A		

2 2	245	
2 2		

▮ ▮	213 (line of demarcation)	
▮ ▮		

**Note: For leaf veins, use four strands of #213 embroidery
floss.**

LUNGWORT *(Pulmonaria)*

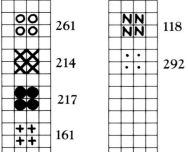

BELLFLOWER
(Campanula persicifolia)

This plant is similar in appearance to the larkspur and the speedwell. It has blue or purple flowers that are either star- or bell-shaped. It blooms between June and August.

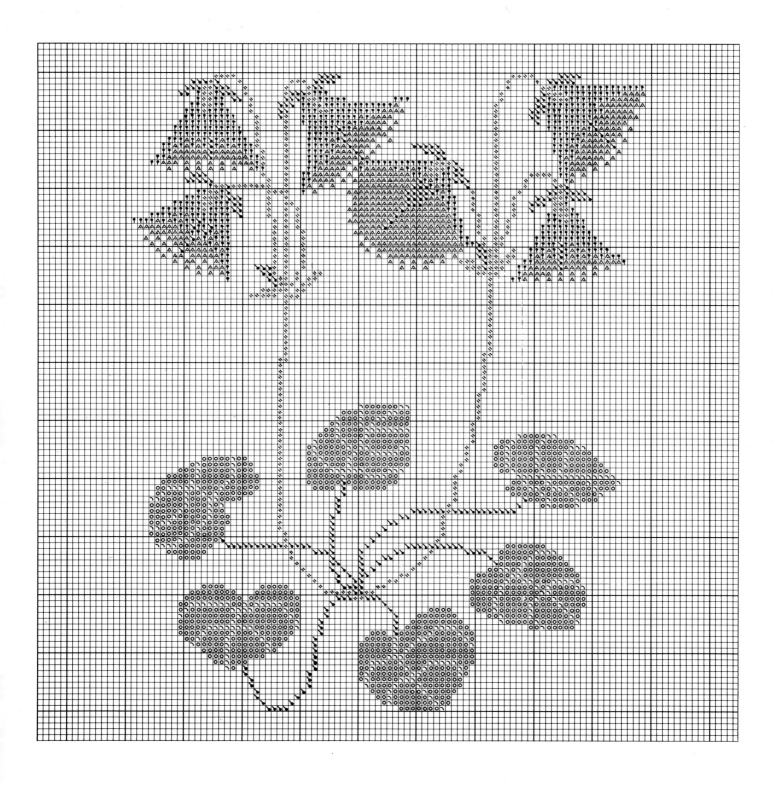

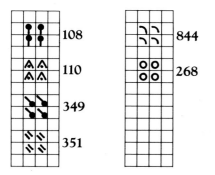

108		844
110		268
349		
351		

This plant is remarkable for its flowers, which droop from the tops of long stems and consist of many feathery petals.

62

MOUNTAIN SNOWBELL *(Soldanella montana)*

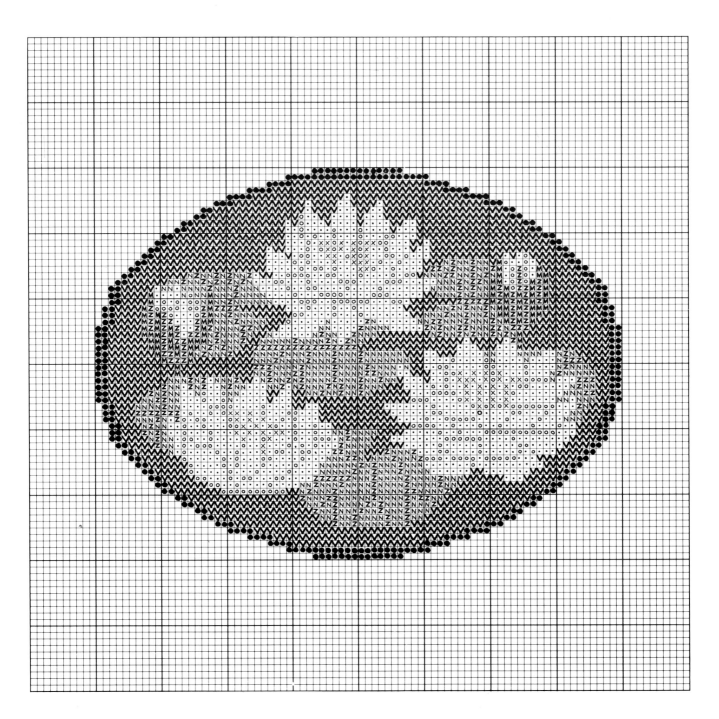

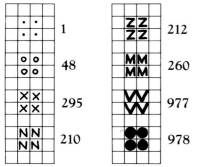

· · / · ·	1	
○ ○ / ○ ○	48	
× × / × ×	295	
N N / N N	210	

Z Z / Z Z	212	
M M / M M	260	
W W / W W	977	
● ● / ● ●	978	

WATER LILY (*Nymphaea alba*)

There is nothing to compare with the sight of a pond whose surface is littered with the fragrant and beautiful blossoms of the water lily. The blooms appear between June and September.

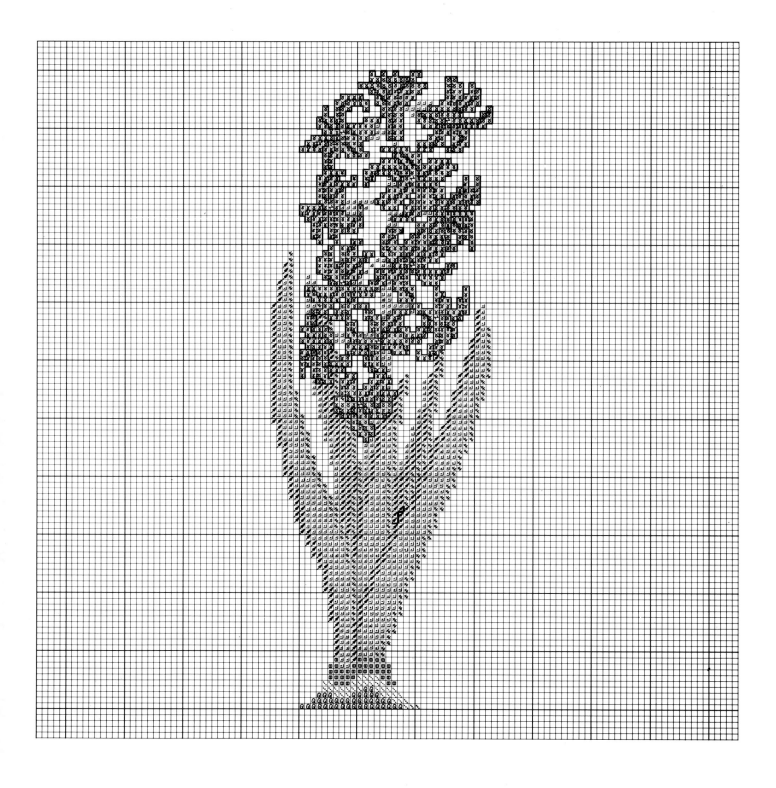

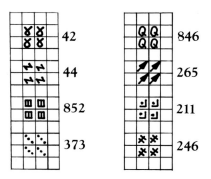

X X / X X	42	
↰↱ / ↲↳	44	
⊞⊞ / ⊞⊞	852	
⸭⸭ / ⸭⸭	373	

QQ / QQ	846	
⫽⫽ / ⫽⫽	265	
⌐⌐ / ⌐⌐	211	
�✻ / ✻✻	246	

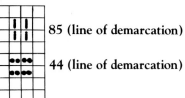

I I	85 (line of demarcation)
•••• ••••	44 (line of demarcation)

Another harbinger of spring, the hyacinth comes in many different varieties, which bloom during April and May.

Note: Use three strands of **#85** embroidery floss for the edges of each flower petal. Also use three strands of **#44** embroidery floss for the stitch in the center of the flower and the lines within the blossoms.

HYACINTH *(Hyacinthus)*

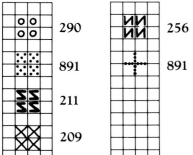

290	
891	
211	
209	

256	
891	

TANSY (*Tanacetum vulgare*)

This plant is commonly known as a weed, but it has an extremely aromatic odor and produces lovely yellow flowers in spring.

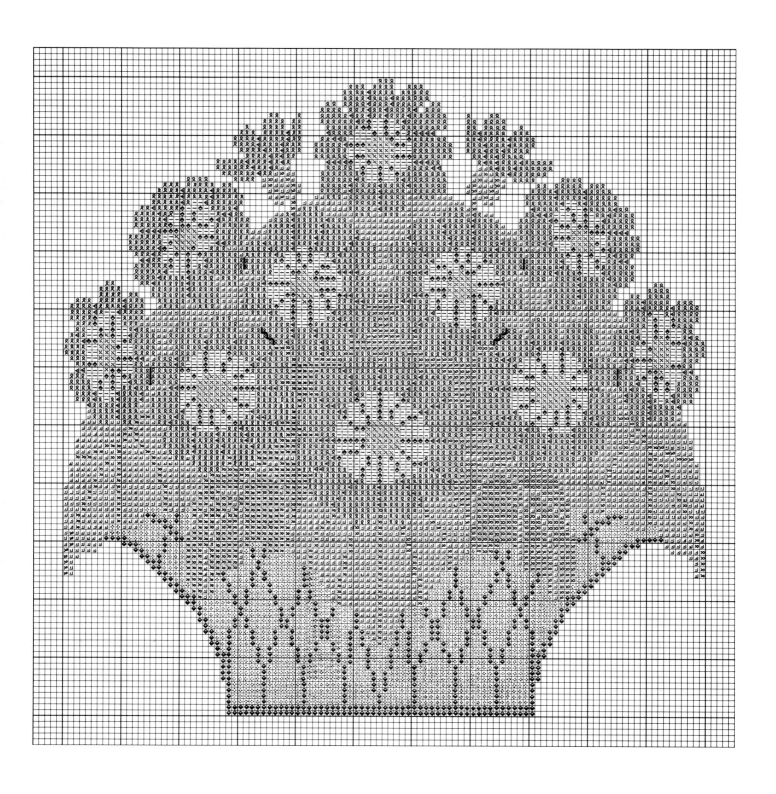

	926
◆◆	887
✕✕	307
┘┘	216

⋈⋈	218
◆◆	399
∴∵	400
ℛℛ	326

◁◁	340
•••	216 (line of demarcation)

This shrub produces bright yellow blossoms in June as long as it is kept in a sheltered but sunny spot.

Note: Use two strands each of #216 and #326 embroidery floss for this project.

CINERARIA *(Senecio cruentus)*

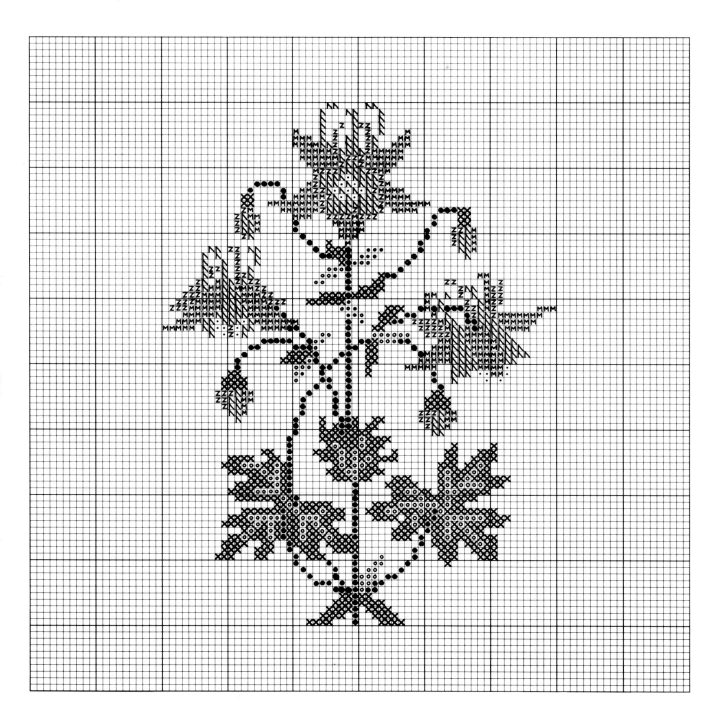

Z Z Z Z	929
M M M M	979
N N N N	149
✕	169

o o o o	433
● ● ● ●	187
· · · ·	926

COLUMBINE
(Aquilegia vulgaris)
This delicate plant is characterized by fernlike leaves and spidery, colorful blossoms, which appear from May to June.

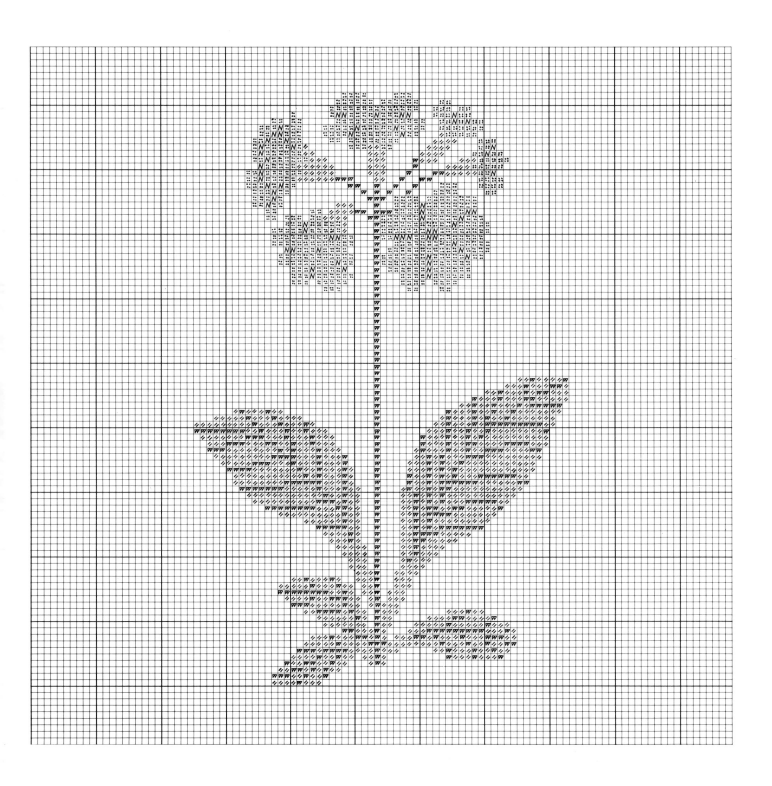

:: :: :: ::	290
N N N N	253
W W W W	255
// // // //	258

This member of the primrose family bears small, bell-shaped, yellow flowers and loves shady, damp soils. It blooms between March and May.

COWSLIP *(Primula veris)*

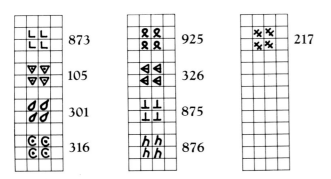

L L / L L	873	⬧ ⬧ / ⬧ ⬧	925	✖ ✖ / ✖ ✖	217
▽ ▽ / ▽ ▽	105	◀ ◀ / ◀ ◀	326		
∂ ∂ / ∂ ∂	301	⊥ ⊥ / ⊥ ⊥	875		
C C / C C	316	♄ ♄ / ♄ ♄	876		

This strange-looking plant has an unpleasant but useful characteristic—it smells bad and so keeps rodents away.

CROWN IMPERIAL FRITILLARIA *(Fritillaria imperialis)*

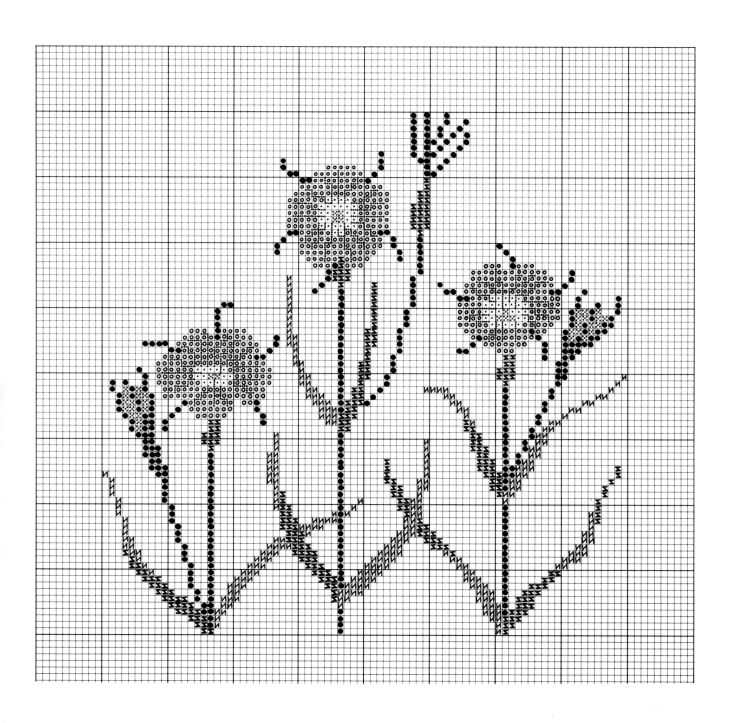

CORNCOCKLE
(Agrostemma githago)

The corncockle is often considered a weed, but it can be a lovely addition to your garden. It is easy to raise and produces a profusion of large flowers throughout late spring and summer.

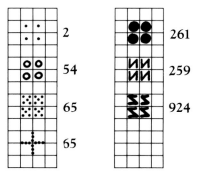

·· / ··	2
oo / oo	54
⋰⋱ / ⋱⋰	65
┼	65

●● / ●●	261
ИИ / ИИ	259
⧄⧄ / ⧄⧄	924

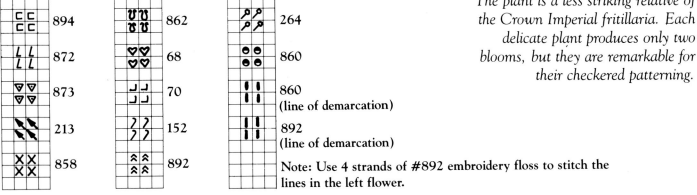

The plant is a less striking relative of the Crown Imperial fritillaria. Each delicate plant produces only two blooms, but they are remarkable for their checkered patterning.

	894
	872
	873
	213
	858

	862
	68
	70
	152
	892

	264
	860
	860 (line of demarcation)
	892 (line of demarcation)

Note: Use 4 strands of #892 embroidery floss to stitch the lines in the left flower.

CHECKERED LILY *(Fritillaria meleagris)*

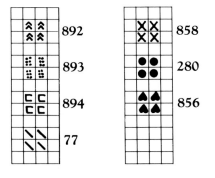

⋩	892
∷	893
⊏	894
＼	77

✕	858
●	280
▲	856

A magnolia tree in full bloom is truly a treat for the eye. The delicately hued blossoms, which have the appearance of fine bone china, appear in March and April.

MAGNOLIA *(Magnolia)*

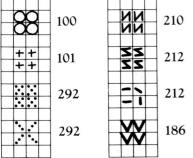

100		210
101		212
292		212
292		186

CLEMATIS *(Clematis hybrida)*

Nicknamed "the queen of the climbers," the clematis vine can create a wall of color when it is in bloom between June and September.

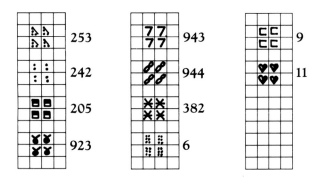

253	943	9
242	944	11
205	382	
923	6	

This ornamental plant is one of the finest of flowering trees. Its large pink or red blossoms cover its branches in April and its fruits appear soon after.

FLOWERING CRABAPPLE *(Malus)*

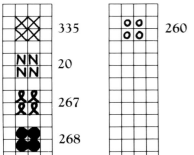

⊠	335
N N / N N	20
🎗🎗 / 🎗🎗	267
●	268

o o / o o	260

FLOWERING TOBACCO
(*Nicotiana sanderae*)

This plant is particularly popular among gardeners because of the wonderful fragrance of its blossoms. Nicotiana flowers between June and October.

⊥⊥ / ⊥⊥	875	KK / KK	303	ΓΓ / ΓΓ	288	QQ / QQ	393
⌡⌡ / ⌡⌡	877	ƷƷ / ƷƷ	279	⚔⚔ / ⚔⚔	291	—/ / —/	338 (antennae)
▷▷ / ▷▷	879	△△ / △△	324	⊖⊖ / ⊖⊖	338	—/ / —/	393 (legs)
⊙⊙ / ⊙⊙	316			⊂⊂ / ⊂⊂	391		

This very rare plant grows only on rocky slopes in mixed woodland environments. It blooms in late spring.

CROWN VETCH *(Coronilla emerus)*

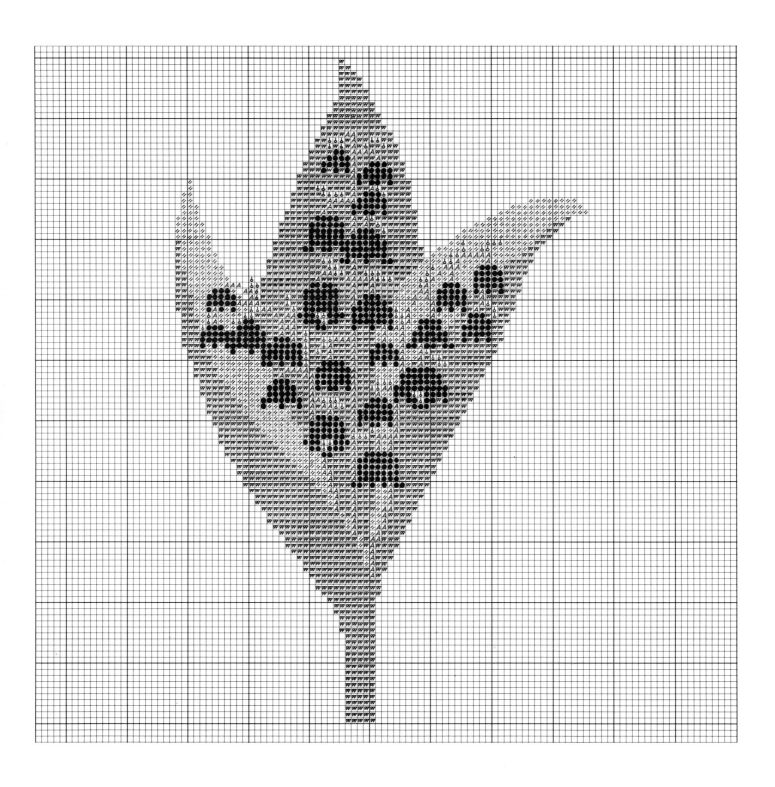

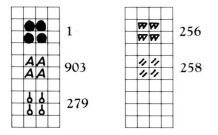

●● ●● ●● ●●	1
AA AA AA AA	903
♦♦ ♦♦ ♦♦ ♦♦	279

₩₩ ₩₩ ₩₩ ₩₩	256
⁄⁄ ⁄⁄ ⁄⁄ ⁄⁄	258

The lily of the valley is not a lily, but it is one of the most attractive of spring flowers. The tiny white blossoms and vivid green leaves appear together in May.

LILY OF THE VALLEY (*Convallaria majalis*)

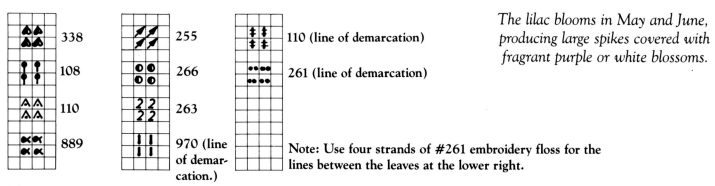

The lilac blooms in May and June, producing large spikes covered with fragrant purple or white blossoms.

338	255	110 (line of demarcation)
108	266	261 (line of demarcation)
110	263	
889	970 (line of demarcation.)	

Note: Use four strands of #261 embroidery floss for the lines between the leaves at the lower right.

LILAC *(Syringa vulgaris)*

⠶ 73	⋁⋁ 255	⋚⋚ 245
⌗ 52	⋈ 267	⬛⬛ 110
⋓⋓ 96	⤙ 267	
❀❀ 98	ии 257	

SWEET PEA
(*Lathyrus odoratus*)
This plant produces a profusion of
brightly colored blossoms between June
and October. Some varieties can grow
as tall as eight feet.

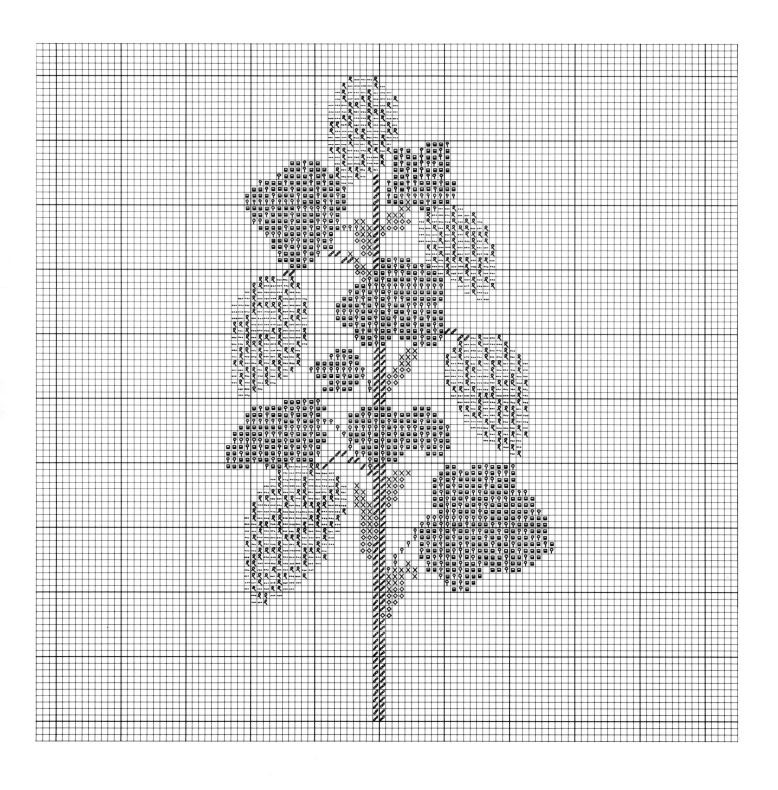

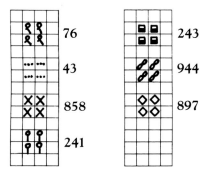

	76		243
	43		944
	858		897
	241		

This native North American shrub has become very popular in Europe since it was first brought there during the early 19th century. Its large, pink blossom heads appear in March or April.

FLOWERING CURRANT *(Ribes rubrum)*

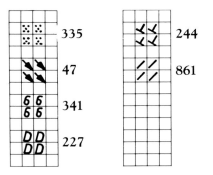

335	244
47	861
341	
227	

Most assuredly one of the most popular garden plants, the geranium comes in a dazzling variety of colors and shapes. They will bloom continuously from spring to fall if provided with sufficient sunlight.

GERANIUM *(Pelargonium zonale)*

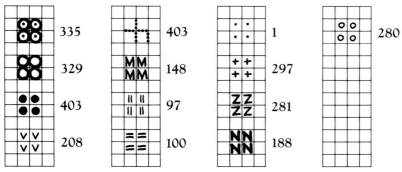

	335		403		1		280
	329	MM	148	++	297		
	403	‖‖	97	ZZ	281		
vv	208	==	100	NN	188		

CORN POPPY
(Papaver rhoeas, red flower)

CORNFLOWER (*Centaurea cyanus*, blue flower)

MUM DAISY (*Chrysanthemum leucanthemum*, white flower)

The flowers contained in this wreath evoke thoughts of fields and cottage gardens. All three plants are in bloom throughout the summer.

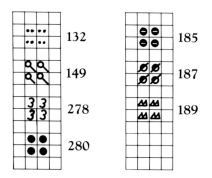

·· ·· / ·· ··	132
॰ ॰ / ॰ ॰	149
3 3 / 3 3	278
● ● / ● ●	280

◒ ◒ / ◒ ◒	185
∅ ∅ / ∅ ∅	187
ᴧ ᴧ / ᴧ ᴧ	189

*The deepest blue variety of this flower
is found only in the Alps, where it
has unfortunately almost disappeared.
It blooms from mid-April to the end
of October.*

GENTIAN (*Gentiana*)

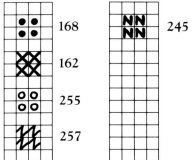

●● ●●	168
⊠	162
○○ ○○	255
⫻	257

NN **NN**	245

FLAX (Linum perenne)

This plant bears an incredible number of blossoms during its flowering period, which lasts from June to August. However, each bloom lasts for only one day.

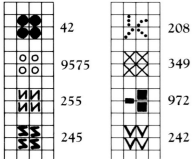

Symbol	Color		Symbol	Color
●	42		⋮	208
○	9575		⊠	349
И	255		■	972
Ƨ	245		W	242

ROSE (*Rosa*)

One of the benefits of having a fragrant flower garden is that it attracts many species of butterfly. Roses are one of the best flowers for this purpose.

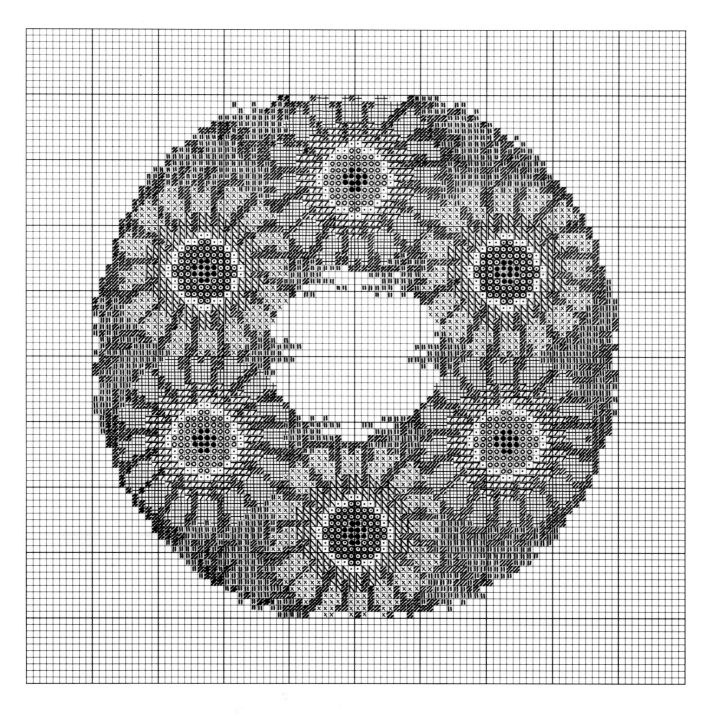

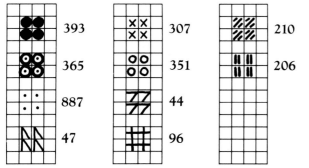

●	393	× ×	307	╱ ╱	210
◉	365	○ ○	351	‖ ‖	206
· ·	887	╱	44		
∖ ∖	47	╫	96		

CHRYSANTHEMUM
(Chrysanthemum carinatum)
This is a rarely grown species of annual chrysanthemum. It flowers from July until November and provides excellent blooms for cut-flower arranging.

INDEX OF PATTERNS